Mr Marvel liked to do magic tricks.

His friend, Squeak, the mouse, liked
to help him.

Mr Marvel tried lots of magic tricks
but they always seemed to go wrong.

One day Mr Marvel wanted a
cake to eat.

'I want a cake,' said Mr Marvel.
'I want a cake too,' said Squeak.

2

'ABRACADABRA!' said Mr Marvel.
'We want a cake.'

'No, no!' said Squeak.
'This is not a cake.'

'No, it is not a cake,'
said Mr Marvel.
'It is a rake.'

'We don't want a rake,'
said Squeak.
'We want a cake.'

6

'ABRACADABRA!' said Mr Marvel.
'We want a cake.'

'Help! Help!' said Squeak.
'This is not a cake.'

'No, it is not a cake,'
said Mr Marvel.
'It is a snake!'

'We don't want a snake.
ABRACADABRA!' said Mr Marvel.
'We want a cake.'

'Here is a cake,' said Squeak.
'Now we can eat it.'

'Oh no!' said Squeak.
'The cake is in the snake!'